We Came A-Marching... 1, 2, 3

Written by MILDRED HOBZEK

Illustrated by WILLIAM PÈNE DU BOIS

PARENTS' MAGAZINE PRESS/NEW YORK

Printed in the United States of America
10 9 8 7 6 5 4 3 2 1

Designed by M. Phillips Kantrowitz

Library of Congress Cataloging in Publication Data

Hobzek, Mildred.
We came a marching, one, two, three.

SUMMARY: Three marching soldiers determine to see the birds in a nest on top of a tall tree. The recurring refrain gives the marching count in twelve different languages.

[1. American poetry] I. Du Bois, William Pène, 1916- II. Title.
PZ8.3.H664We 398.8 78-7793
ISBN 0-8193-0974-5
ISBN 0-8193-0975-3 lib. bdg.

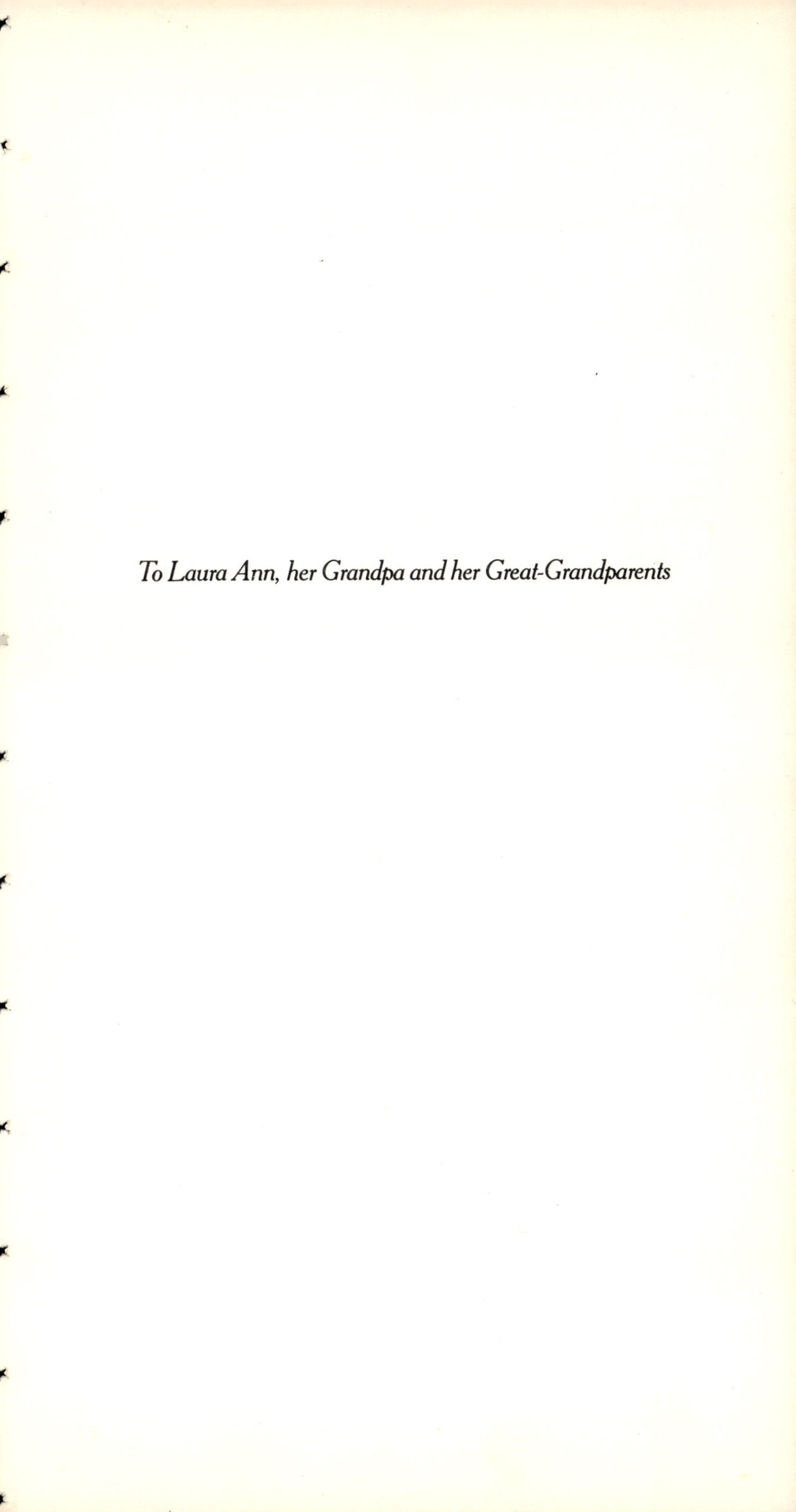

To Laura Ann, her Grandpa and her Great-Grandparents

AUTHOR'S NOTE

Counting in a language other than their own has been a source of delight to many children. This adaptation of a rollicking old German tale, set to a Slavic folk song, provides an opportunity to sing "one, two, three," in twelve languages, occidental and oriental.

Language origin is indicated on each page by flags of the respective countries. Phonetic pronunciation of the numbers is printed in color in the repeat phrase of each verse, with the accented syllable in capital letters.

Pronunciations have been verified by the language specialists in the Foreign Literature Department and the John G. White Department of Folklore, Orientalia and Chess of the Cleveland Public Library. The song of *We Came A-Marching... One, Two, Three* which appears at the end, is sung in a brisk march tempo, with gusto!

—Mildred Hobzek

ENGLISH

On a sunny morning,
We were called for duty.
We came a-marching, one, two, three,
Sacha, Stanislav and me—

We came a-marching, one, two, three,
Sacha, Stanislav and me!

GERMAN

Guard your great King's forest,
Were the captain's orders.
So we are marching, eins, zwei, drei,
Sacha, Stanislav and I—

So we are marching, īns, tsvī, drī,*
Sacha, Stanislav and I.

*use long "i" sound, as in write

FRENCH

Sacha spied a large bird
Circling high above us...
We kept a-marching, un, deux, trois,
Sacha, Stanislav et moi—

We kept a-marching, ûh, deuh, trwah,
Sacha, Stanislav ay mwah.

RUSSIAN

Soaring to a treetop
Where his nest was hidden,
We followed marching, adín, dva, tri,
Sacha, Stanislav and me—

We followed marching, ah-DʸEEN, dvah, tree,
Sacha, Stanislav and me.

DUTCH

Looking up, we heard them
Peeping oh so gaily!
We stopped our marching, een, twee, drie,
Sacha, Stanislav and me—

We stopped our marching, en,* tveh, dree
Sacha, Stalislav and me.

**en, use short "e" sound, as in* met

POLISH

We must see those birdies,
But we had no ladder.
How could we do it, jeden, dwa, trzy,
Sacha, Stanislav and me—

How could we do it, YEH-den, dvah, tshee,
Sacha, Stanislav and me.

WELSH

Just then came a woodsman,
Simple, strong and sturdy.
We'll hop up on him, un, dau, tri,
Sacha, Stanislav and me—

We'll hop up on him, EE-un, dī,* tree,
Sacha, Stanislav and me.

**di, use long "i" sound, as in* write

BULGARIAN

So we formed a ladder
Tall enough to reach them,
Shaking, swaying, edno, dve, tri,
Sacha, Stanislav and me—

Shaking, swaying, eh-DNO, dveh, tree,
Sacha, Stanislav and me.

URDU

The Language of Pakistan.

At the top, bold Sacha
Shouted down, "They're beauties!
Great big babies, aik, do, teen,
Birds like these you've never seen—

Great big babies, aik, dō*, teen,
Birds like these you've never seen!"

*aik, *as in* take; *dō, as in* dough

GAELIC-IRISH

Woodsman stepped out shouting,
"I must see those birdies!"
Down we tumbled, a haon, a dó, a trí,
Sacha, Stanislav and me.

Down we tumbled—a HAYn , a daw, a tree,
Sacha, Stanislav and me.

SPANISH

Give three cheers for bravery,
Though we're bruised and battered,
Stalwart soldiers, uno, dos, tres,
Clever fellows, we confess—

Stalwart soldiers, OO-noh, dohs, trehs,
Clever fellows, we confess.

JAPANESE

Guard the great King's forest,
Those were still our orders.
So we are marching, ichi, ni, san,
One foot up and one foot down—

So we are marching, EE-chee, nee, sahn,
One foot up and one foot down!

Stalwart soldiers, one, two, three,
Sacha, Stanislav and me.

We came a-marching, one, two, three,

Old Slavic Song

March tempo (in 2)

C F C

On a sun-ny morn-ing We were call'd for du-ty,

G7 C G7 C

We came a-mar-ching one, two, three, Sa-cha, Sta-ni-slav and me-

F C G7 C

We came a-mar-ching one, two, three, Sa-cha, Sta-ni-slav and me!